THE PATH

Learning the Ways of God

GRANT CRARY

THE PATH
Learning the Ways of God
by Grant Crary

Copyright © 2023 Grant Crary. All rights reserved.

ISBN: 978-0-9982243-4-3

Design by Brett Burner

All scripture is taken from the New King James Version. Copyright © 1982 by Thomas Nelson, Inc. All rights reserved. Used by permission.

Printed in the United States of America.

Published by:
Fairdale Publishing
www.fairdalepublishing.com

No part of this publication may be reproduced, stored in a retrieval system, or transmitted in any form, or by any means, electronic, mechanical, including photocopy, recording, or by any informational storage and retrieval system, without the prior, written permission of the publisher. Please direct permission requests and other correspondences to Fairdale Publishing (fairdalepublishing.com).

Dedication

This book is dedicated to my wife, Jillian, who has been my friend and companion throughout our life together. Her wisdom, kindness, encouragement, and love for the Lord are a priceless blessing.

Contents

Introduction vii

1. WHAT DO WE MEAN BY "WAYS"? 1

2. WHAT ARE THE WAYS OF GOD? 9

3. UNDERLYING PRINCIPLES 21

4. HOW CAN WE LEARN THE WAYS OF GOD? 31

5. SOME THINGS THAT GOD VALUES 41

6. EXAMPLES 55

7. WHY WAS MOSES DIFFERENT? 67

Introduction

As a young Christian in my late teens, I read the Bible extensively, and that has been extremely beneficial throughout my life. One day, I was reading Psalm 103, and the seventh verse stood out to me. It says, "He made known His ways to Moses, His acts to the children of Israel." I could see that Moses was on a different plane from the rest of the people, which is confirmed in the account of the journey from Egypt to the plains on the east side of the river Jordan in the territory of Moab, just before Israel crossed into the Promised Land. The difference is summed up succinctly in this verse in Psalm 103. The people saw what God did. He provided food, water, guidance, shade, warmth…everything that they needed to survive in the harsh desert conditions. Moses, however, was different. Not only did he see what God did, but he also understood how God thought, what was the motivation behind His actions, what were His ways. His relationship with God was entirely different.

The thought of understanding God's ways has challenged me ever since I first read this passage in Psalm 103.

In Isaiah 55:8, we read that God declares that His ways are not the same as ours. Most of us have little dispute with that statement and have known times when God answered a prayer in an entirely different way compared to how we expected, but His solution was so much wiser. Or perhaps we have experienced a circumstance that puzzles us, and we don't know why God did not act in a different manner, or even act at all. Sometimes the reasons become clear with time, but sometimes not. Growing in our understanding of God's ways is part of growing into a closer walk with Him. I don't know that we can ever fully understand Him, simply because of the greatness of God, but we can and must continue to grow.

In this book, we will look at aspects that I have learned of His ways, although I am very aware that I have much more to learn. We will examine the underlying key to understanding His ways, which is to understand His nature. He is good through and through, incapable of evil, and He loves us dearly. We must know this if we are to grow in our relationship with Him. The book also has some examples of how God thinks differently from us so we can see the practical outworking of His ways. Sometimes we don't understand why He does something, or allows something to happen, but I am convinced that we will one day find that He was perfectly fair and perfectly just and perfectly wise. I am grateful that I have learned these attributes of God, and it is such joy to be able share what He has taught me.

WHAT DO WE MEAN BY "WAYS"?

The expression, "the ways of God," is found in many different books of the Bible, as too is the use of the term "ways" in relation to people. So, what do we mean by this expression? There are several uses of the word in our language and primarily they relate to a direction that someone takes.

An applicable dictionary definition in the context of the ways of God and the ways of people is, "A personal manner of behaving, acting, or doing." This is a good definition because it combines behaviors with the personal and individual aspects of those behaviors.

We all have certain characteristics pertaining to how we conduct our life, which in a sense, identify us and are unique to us. There are some things that are particularly important to us and other things that we do not regard as being all that important. For example, for some people, physical fitness is very important, whereas it may be considered of value but not as important to others. Attaining position and recognition is important to some people, but again, not so to others. Status symbols, honesty, work ethic, popularity, family, entertainment, education…all these and many other aspects of life hold varying degrees of importance to us, and the sum of all these characteristics identifies us. It is how we think, how we live our life, our moral standards, where we invest our time, how we spend our money. These are our individual ways.

In a similar fashion, the ways of God are how He thinks and how He acts. And if we are to grow beyond an elementary level in our Christian life, we must grow in our understanding of God's ways. The apostle John classified Christians into three categories, namely little children, young men, and fathers (1 John 2:12-14). He was using natural human development as an analogy of Christian growth and maturity. Just as there is a considerable difference in the capabilities of children and young adults in natural life, so too did John describe a considerable difference in their spiritual life. The children know that they have received the Lord Jesus, they are saved and have a basic understanding of God. However, the young men are described as being strong, having the word of God abiding in them, and having overcome the devil in their life. Obviously, the young men have progressed well beyond the level of the little children.

It is important that we do not settle for an elementary walk with God, something akin to remaining as children. A child's outlook on life is very limited, and essentially children are concerned with having their own needs met. But as we grow older, we become capable of taking on responsibilities, our physical and mental capabilities are considerably more developed, and our lives become much more productive. The apostle John, under the guidance of the Holy Spirit, gave us this illustration to help us see the importance of growing in our Christian walk. And growth could be stated in terms of our ways becoming more like God's ways.

Returning to John's illustration, we see that while there is a considerable gap between children and young men, the gap between young men and fathers may not be as great. Both are of an age where they are physically and mentally developed, and consequently, they have comparable abilities. So, what do fathers have over young men? Basically, it is wisdom and experience, gleaned from having lived longer and grappling with decisions and trials in life. They are in a position to guide the children and young men so that their abilities are utilized productively, and to help them make wise decisions. I believe that if we can become a spiritual young man, there is a strong possibility that we can advance to becoming a spiritual father. What is important then, is that we do not remain as children but progress at least the level of the young men.

Let us consider the qualities that John listed as being applicable to spiritual young men.

1. They are strong.

In Ephesians 4:14 the apostle Paul wrote, "That we should no longer be children, tossed to and fro and carried about with every wind of doctrine, in the trickery of men, by the cunning craftiness of deceitful plotting." One who is strong in this sense has a solid foundation. They understand right from wrong; they are not vulnerable to being taken in by teachings and practices that are actually contrary to God. They are able to set a wise direction and make sound decisions because they are well grounded.

At our church, some members of our staff regularly receive emailed requests, purportedly from our lead pastor, to send money to some organization. However, because we know the pastor, we quickly recognize that the messages are not how he writes, and we do not respond because we see that the messages are fraudulent. Were we to follow the directions of the email, we would be sending money to a thief. One could say that in this area we are strong, and that we understand the ways of our lead pastor. We know him, his mannerisms, his choice of words, the way he phrases his conversation, and the type of requests that he would make. Consequently, we are not fooled. (As an aside, it is important for a staff to be good stewards of church funds because those monies have been donated. The funds need to be protected and used wisely.)

2. The word of God abides in them.

There are two aspects to this admonition. Firstly, we have to regularly read our Bibles so that we know what is written. The Bible presents revelation and information regarding the character of God, who He is, what He is like, what are His ways. Secondly, we have to be doers, not just hearers (James 1:22-25). If we are to move on from being spiritual children, we must have the word of God within us. The apostle Peter stated that the scriptures were written under the leading of the Holy Spirit, and that they are divinely inspired (2 Peter 1:20-21). We don't just have to take Peter's word for it because this statement has been confirmed to be true by mathematical evaluation.

It is a sad fact that too many Christians read their Bibles infrequently. We can learn from listening to messages and reading books, but our most valuable source of input of truth comes from our own personal Bible reading. Without a sound knowledge of Bible principles, and our living our lives according to the light and understanding that God has made known to us, we will remain spiritual children.

3. They have overcome the evil one.

The evil one was defeated by Jesus through His death on the cross, and this enables us to have victory in our own lives too. These victories may be seen in overcoming sin, in changing bad habits, and having the fruit of the Spirit (Galatians 5:22-23) evident in our lives. In the context of our being in conflict with the devil and his followers, we should consider the armor of God, listed by the apostle Paul in Ephesians 6:13-18. Very briefly:

- **The belt of truth.** A belt holds other garments together and provides a way to carry items of importance. If we do not know the truth of the Bible, or we practice deceit in our lives, we have nothing with which to hold our life together. Consider a police officer. The officer's belt holds several vital pieces of equipment that are necessary for the work – firearm, taser, baton, handcuffs, radio, flashlight, and probably other items as well. That belt is an essential piece of their equipment. Just as we too are facing conflict, we must have the belt of truth.

- **Breastplate of righteousness.** A breastplate protected the soldier's vital organs. Things that are vital to our spiritual life, and sometimes our natural life too, are only safe if we walk righteously, which is to live rightly, according to His commands. When we looked at the belt of truth, we considered how necessary a belt is to a police officer. An officer also has a breastplate, the protective vest. These are made of Kevlar, which is very strong. I worked for a company that made containment cases for commercial aircraft engines. These cases are giant aluminum rings, and the fan blades rotate within them. They are designed so that if a blade breaks, it will be "contained" in the engine and not take the plane down. Interestingly, the rings are wrapped with a material…Kevlar. And if a blade breaks, it may penetrate the ring, but it will not pass through the Kevlar. It is a "breastplate" to protect the aircraft from disaster, just like the Kevlar vest protects an officer from bullets.

- **Feet shod with the gospel of peace.** The feet represent our walk, and our overriding purpose in life needs to be in some way leading people into a closer walk with God. It also means that our focus is primarily on eternal things, not on the things of this earth. This does not mean that we have to become evangelists, but rather that our life is a demonstration of God being in it. People who we interface with regularly observe us and may come to us in their difficult times. In my family, I was the first Christian and the other family members did not heed my testimony to follow the Lord. However, I found that when they experienced difficulties they would inevitably ask me for my prayers. This was surprising because they were the ones with more of life's experiences, whereas I was only in my twenties, but they recognized something in my life that they needed.

- **The shield of faith.** Faith is not a blind leap in God's direction. Faith is something that the Holy Spirit imparts to us, and while it often involves stepping into unknown territory, it is grounded in the knowledge of God's character and of His guiding in the matter. The better we know God, the greater the faith we can exercise. This is the same as our relationship with people. We understand and trust those we know well and have found to be reliable, but in the case of strangers have not proved their character to us, our trust will be given much more cautiously, if at all.

- **The helmet of salvation.** Most of our spiritual battles are fought in our minds. A quote that is attributed to Henry Ford says, "If you think you can do something you are probably right, and if you think you cannot do something you are probably right." Therefore, our mind needs to be protected by a sound knowledge of what Jesus accomplished for us on the cross, how we no longer have to be subject to sin, how we can overcome fears and trials in our life, and what a great reward awaits us in heaven. Guarding our mind is so very important. We need to be careful what we watch and what we read and what we hear.

- **The sword of the Spirit.** Paul specifically tells us that this is the Word of God, the Bible. We need to know it in our hearts and understanding, and live it out in our words and actions. The Bible can be like a weapon that we wield because the devil hates the truth. And truth sets us free.

- **Prayer.** Most of us find it difficult to pray for any length of time, but if we recognize that prayer is talking with God, just as conversation is talking with people, perhaps it will not be so difficult. Lofty words are not required. We should share our life with Him, and ask Him to accomplish things, both in our own life and in accordance with His purposes on the earth. We need to make prayer a natural part of our day.

When we consider the young men and how they have overcome the evil one, that might appear impossible to us. After all, we are not bigger, stronger, or smarter than the devil. However, we are nevertheless able to overcome through what Jesus did for us on the cross. His blood was shed to provide the way for forgiveness of sin and restoration of relationship with God. We overcome through identifying with Him and His victory, by the life that we lead, and by our complete commitment to Him regardless of the consequences (Revelation 12:11). Overcoming sin and trials in our life are a sign of spiritually maturing.

How we behave, act, and conduct ourselves; these are our ways. And God has His ways too. The aim for us is that we would understand His ways, and that they would influence our life so that we are not only changed more and more into the likeness of His character, but also that we would ˆ His plan for our lives.

WHAT ARE THE WAYS OF GOD?

We saw that a good definition of a person's ways is, "A personal manner of behaving, acting, or doing." A person's ways then, are individual and unique to each person. They reflect the kind of person that someone is, what is important to that person, and how they express themselves. We want to grow closer to God, and to do so, we need to understand His ways, understand what is important to Him. We will proceed to look at some of the ways of God. Obviously, this book cannot remotely cover all of God's ways, even if we could be capable of knowing them. However, we will discuss some aspects of how He thinks and how He acts. We will not specifically look at His character, although His character is interwoven with everything He does, but focus on how He thinks and how He acts.

A summary of what should be our focus
One of many passages in the Bible that gives us insight into His ways is found in Jeremiah 9:23-24, which says, "Let not

the wise man glory in his wisdom, let not the mighty man glory in his might, nor let the rich man glory in his riches; but let him who glories, glory in this, that he knows and understands Me, that I am the Lord, exercising lovingkindness, judgment, and righteousness in the earth, for in these I delight, says the Lord."

What can we learn from this passage? Firstly, God lists three things that we are not to glory in, and by "glory" we mean something to be proud of, or something that causes us to appear important in our own estimation of ourselves. We must always remember that any talent that we have, our abilities and everything about us, has been given to us. We must have a humble realization that these all come from the good and generous hand of God. So, when He says not to be proud of our wisdom, or perhaps we could say our intellect and knowledge, we need to recognize that this has been given to us by One who is infinitely wiser and more intelligent than ourselves. It is easy to consider ourselves to be superior to others if we have an intellect that understands complex things, enables us to speak well, and other qualities associated with intellect. However, if we are intelligent, we are not to think that this makes us better than others but instead to use our intelligence wisely. There are many people who were very intelligent but also made very unwise decisions. Wisdom is more valuable than intelligence.

The second point is not to be proud of our might. This could refer to physical strength, perhaps to good looks, or to our position in life such as the job that we hold. These are things that help our life on earth and make things easier for us, but they do not impress God. Good looks and outstanding skills impress people, but God looks for character. People might look up to us, giving honor and even paying homage to us, but we are not to be prideful of our abilities or develop a swelled head. If we are given a job that has greater responsibility and a better title than someone else, we must humbly thank God and use it effectively and wisely.

Thirdly, we are not to be proud of riches. As with the previous two subjects, it is very easy to consider ourselves superior to others if we have more money and better material things. But how did we obtain them? We may have worked hard to get them, but it is God who enables us to receive them and creates the opportunities for us. And like the previous two subjects, if material prosperity is our main focus then we are on the wrong path in life. I read a quote from a wealthy man, speaking from his own experience, who I don't believe had a Christian walk at that time. Nevertheless, I thought he summed wealth up very succinctly when he said, "Money doesn't buy happiness, but it does make life easier." Again, our focus must be on eternal things so that the things that make this life easier are secondary. Not unimportant, but secondary.

In His kindness, God then presents the path that we should be on, the place where our focus and "ambition" in life should lie. That path is to know and understand Him, and that requirement in itself should keep us humble because when we compare ourselves to Him, we quickly realize that there really is no comparison. We are like Job, who after God had presented him with forty-two questions to which he had no answer, Job's reply was one of utter humility, saying that God had said things that were "too wonderful for me, which I did not know." (Job 42:1-6).

In our passage from Jeremiah 9, God then proceeds to summarize His attributes, the aspects of His character that He delights to see in us. When we follow them, we can come to know and understand Him. To know and understand God is to understand His ways, so these attributes are important for us. They are:

    a. **He is the Lord.** Simply put, He has no equal, no competitor. It is essential that we live under this knowledge, humbly seeking to please Him in all that we do and in what we say and how we think. All aspects of our life are to be governed by obedience to His commands.

    b. **His lovingkindness.** God is good, through and through. He is absolutely pure, absolutely wise. Furthermore, His love for us is astonishing. Consequently, He disciplines us when we need it, and uses all the things that come into our life to help us grow closer to Him, which will result if we walk through them with the right attitude. As the apostle John wrote, "God is love," and if we do not love we cannot know God. (1 John 4:8).

    c. **His judgments.** We all have a sense of the need for justice. This is reflected in our laws, in prison sentences, and fines for wrongdoing. In this we are like God, for He also executes justice. Very often, it is tempered with His kindness and mercy, and very often it is delayed by His desire that we would turn from our unrighteous path and live as we should, in accordance with His commands. One day we will have to stand before the Lord to give an account of our lives and I am very sure that no one will be able to say that His judgment is unfair. In His love, God also executes justice.

d. **His Righteousness.** We could say that lovingkindness and judgment speak of the "book ends" of the nature of God. So, what governs these character aspects? What is it about Him that causes these attributes to be so perfect? It is His righteousness. Everything He does is right, even though we might not understand. It is essential that we be thoroughly grounded in this truth. Our perspective of an event is limited by the facts that are before us, but God sees beyond that and as Isaiah wrote, He knows the end of a matter from its beginning (Isaiah 46:10).

The Ten Commandments

When God gave the Ten Commandments, and other instructions in the law, it was something unique among the nations. Israel would have a set of laws by which they would govern themselves. These laws were not the changing whims of a king but wise instruction from the all-wise God. In those laws we can see His mercy and His justice, as mentioned in the passage from Jeremiah above, and they became the basis for the legal systems of western nations such as the United States. For example, in the law there was provision for a person who had fallen on hard times to have a fresh start with the forgiveness of debts every seven years, and this principle has been incorporated into our laws regarding bankruptcy so that a person can have the opportunity to recover from a financial setback.

The Ten Commandments embodied the law, and it is fair to say that most of those commands can be found in the laws of the various cultures of our world. Respect for parents, faithfulness in marriage, respect for other people's belongings, honesty in legal proceedings, not committing murder, not committing theft…these are all things that instinctively we know to be right and important, even if the laws relating to them are lax, and they are all important in most, if not all cultures. We will do well to contemplate the implications of the Ten Commandments. They set forth values that God holds, and our failure to live by them will hinder our being able to know Him.

The summary of the Law

In Matthew 22:36-40 we read how one day, a teacher of the law approached Jesus and asked Him, "What is the great commandment in the law?" The man was testing Jesus, probably hoping that when Jesus elevated one particular commandment above the others, perhaps the command not to be an idolater, He would be criticized for not mentioning some other commandment such as not committing murder. However, Jesus answered him with wisdom, and actually summarized the entire law in just two points – love God and love your fellow man. Jesus said that all of the law and the teaching of the prophets, in other words the entire Bible of that day, was based on these commandments. In fact, when we consider the New Testament, we realize that it is also all about the same two commands.

In our present age, it is fair to say that loving God and loving other people are considered secondary to loving ourselves, and so we should look closer to the actual words of Jesus. Regarding our having a love for God, He said that we should love Him with all our heart, soul, and mind. This is a high standard indeed. But God is utterly worthy of this standard. Our love for God must come from the center of our being and our desires in life. It is demonstrated in our decisions and our emotions, and in the way we think. In other words, we are to love God with our entire being from our very core.

This presents the question of what does loving God look like? We tend to use the word "love" very loosely, ranging from our affection for people to our favorite hamburger and everything in between. However, the apostle John gave us a simple yardstick by which to measure our love for God – keeping His commandments (1 John 5:3).

So, if our love for God depends on our keeping His commands, how are we different from the Pharisees of Jesus' day? After all, they were meticulous in keeping the law (as they had interpreted it). And yet, Jesus said if our righteousness does not exceed theirs, we will not see the kingdom of heaven (Matthew 5:20). That statement should grab our attention!

The Pharisees had a list of rules to keep, things that they must do or not do, and they considered that adhering to their list of rules demonstrated their righteousness. However, Jesus had very harsh words for them. He called them hypocrites, blind guides, fools, whitewashed tombs, and lawless people. The reason for His denunciation of them was clearly stated when He said, "You cleanse the outside of the cup and dish, but inside they are full of extortion and self-indulgence."

I had an instance to seriously consider this statement about the inside and the outside of a cup. I was performing some short-term missionary work in another country, and we came to a certain home. These homes were not like ours but constructed with poor materials and had cow dung floors. These were poor people but nevertheless, they were hospitable and always welcomed strangers with a bowl of tea. As we approached a particular home, the mother called to her daughter (we spoke through interpreters and not knowing the language I could not understand what was said) and the girl whisked an enamel bowl away from a dog who was drinking out of it. Presently, when our tea was served, I was positive that I recognized my bowl as being the one that was also used for the dog's water. It had certain chips out of the rim and there was rust showing in several places. I thought to myself, "It's what is in the cup that matters, not the chips and rust on the outside." And I drank my tea...

So, we are faced with John's statement that keeping God's commands demonstrates our love for Him, and yet the Pharisees who diligently kept the law were denounced by Jesus. What is the difference? Jesus was not impressed by the Pharisees' legalistic keeping of rules because it came from self-effort and not from the heart. Worse still, their hearts were corrupt, motivated by greed and ambition. What makes the difference is that when we commit ourselves to Jesus, asking Him into our life, He changes us on the inside. The Pharisees' "righteousness" was entirely based on their works, but they were corrupt on the inside. Without Jesus in our life, we have no more ability to be truly righteous from the heart than the Pharisees, but the marvelous truth is that Jesus changes us on the inside. We have to apply ourselves to live as He instructed us, but He enables us by changing our heart (Hebrews 8:10). The laws of God are then developed within us, not a set of rules to try to keep. We are changed. This is the miracle of the new birth – we are born again by the Spirit of God.

Of course, we do have to cooperate with God for His laws to be written in our heart. He enables us, but we have to do our part too. As Paul wrote in Romans, we have to present the members of our body as instruments of righteousness, not unrighteousness (Romans 6:13). For example, God has instructed that sexual relations be reserved for marriage, not before and not with others after we have married. Some have said, "We are committed to each other and will be married soon. What is the problem with our enjoying sexual relations before our marriage?" This reasoning does seem plausible because the couple are committed to marrying so it is not like they are being promiscuous or committing adultery. However, here is the crux of the matter. Jesus asked us to refrain until we are actually married. If we love Him, we will keep His commandments and not interject our own desires.

Looking at the end of a matter

One of the aspects of God is how He knows everything, including things that have not yet taken place. This is because He is not bound by time as we are on earth, and simply because He is God. There is nothing that escapes His knowledge or attention. This, of course, is why predestination is not some arbitrary, unfair selection that He makes, choosing one person and passing over another. Predestination is governed by His foreknowledge, as the Apostle Paul wrote in Romans 8:29.

God's foreknowledge is apparent in the Bible prophecies. A significant portion of the Bible contains prophecies, which is something that sets the Bible apart from any other book. Many of them have already been fulfilled, while some pertain to periods in history which we have not yet reached. It is not surprising that there are many prophecies, nor is it surprising that they have been fulfilled, because God knows everything, even future events, and it was the Holy Spirit who authored the Bible through the various writers. Predicting the future is not problematical to Someone who knows it in advance.

God's ability to know the future affects our personal lives too. There are times when we have prayed, asking God to do a certain thing and He does not do it. We are disappointed, perhaps wondering why He did not answer our request when it seemed to be such a sensible solution to the problem. However, later we find that God solved the problem in a different way which turned out to be better than our solution, or we find that by having to walk through the situation rather than have it solved, some other objective was accomplished, possibly something that we had not even considered. One example that I encountered occurred in my workplace some years ago. I was under a group of people who were tight knit and often went drinking together. If one was not part of that group, one felt vulnerable and I really wondered what the future held for me. I began to consider seeking employment elsewhere and praying that God would open a new door for me. To my surprise, God had a different solution. In a short space of time, some of them were transferred to other divisions, or promoted out of the area. The atmosphere was completely changed, and the vacuum that the departures created led to a promotion for me that was to set the path for the remainder of my career. God answered my prayer, not by finding a new employer for me but by changing the conditions at my current place of employment and in the process setting me up for the rest of my working days.

There are two important qualities about God that we need to keep in mind.

1. As Isaiah wrote, He knows the end of a matter from its beginning (Isaiah 46:10).

2. As Jeremiah wrote, God is wise beyond any understanding of mankind (Jeremiah 10:7).

When we put these two qualities together, we see that with wisdom and foresight, God orchestrates events to bring about His purposes in the end. We can see only as far as is visible to us while we are passing through this difficult time, but He sees the end. As a result, we must live our lives in full assurance of His goodness. We will undoubtedly have to face difficulties, perhaps even tragedies, but God is good and, "All things work together for good to those who love God..." (Romans 8:28).

Being a Father

Jesus constantly referred to God as His Father. While this might appear obvious when Jesus is called the Son (of God), there is more to the title than just the position. "Father" would appear to be the highest title in the universe. In reference to our walk with God, it is not so much addressing His creative works, although that would be appropriate. Rather, it is addressing our relationship with Him.

In the very best sense of the word, God is a father. Earthly fathers take responsibility for their family. They care for their children, attending to the needs and often to their wants as well. They seek to guide the children into a lifestyle and a career that would be good and rewarding, relative to the individual child's skills and interests. They love their children. In love, a father also corrects his children, and God knows it is not loving to let us go our own way. He knows what is right for us and will bring about circumstances so that we change our direction and do as He says, do what is actually in our own best interests. And when someone touches His children, God says, "Vengeance is Mine, I will repay, says the Lord" (Hebrews 10:9).

There is something within us that desires to have a true father. I grew up without my father, my parents having separated when I was a baby and my father being killed a few years later. I never knew him. When my mom remarried, just before I turned nine, I was so excited. At last, I would have a father. Unfortunately, my joy was short-lived because it certainly did not work out that way. The five years we spent with him were terrible, but my point is that having a father was a desire deep within me. It is very comforting that the God of the universe, all-powerful, all-knowing, all-wise, wants us to know Him as Father. He takes interest in the details of our life, observes all that we do and think, and seeks to direct us onto the path that is right for us. In the very best sense, God is our Father.

UNDERLYING PRINCIPLES

In many aspects of life, there is a need to understand certain basic principles in order to perform at a higher standard. Mathematics is a good example, because there is a continual building of one understanding upon another, starting with simple addition and subtraction, until complex problems can be solved in civil engineering, aerospace, and many other fields where human life can be at stake. Very often, to understand something, we need to know the principles that form the foundation for that understanding, the basic building blocks.

The ways of God have their underlying principles too. If we want to know His ways, there are certain other things that we have to understand in order to form the correct foundation in our thinking. Here are some of these.

The Christian life is primarily about God, not about us

This may be a revolutionary statement to some of us, at least in terms of our behaviors, if not in our thinking. While it is true that God loves us so very much, and there are many promises in the Bible about His care for us, the bottom line is that we are created not just for fellowship with Him but for His glory.

We noted in an earlier chapter that a child thinks mainly about having his/her needs met. It is as we grow older that we think more of others. If we are to grow in our closeness to God and understand His ways, we likewise have to realize that the relationship that we have with Him is more about Him than it is about us.

Let us look at some passages from the Bible that illustrate this. In Revelation 4:8-11, we have a description of the activity around the throne of God, and it is all about worshiping Him. We find that the twenty-four elders and the four living creatures are constantly engaged in worship. It is their focus, and the elders, who appear to be people who have been saved by the blood of Jesus, cast their crowns before the throne in recognition that all they are and all they achieved is due to Him. There is no sense of receiving, only of giving. We find the same situation in chapter five where a huge multitude of angels are worshiping the Lamb (Revelation 5:11-12).

Some people have the attitude that God should be like a genie in a flask, and if we give the flask a few rubs, He will appear and answer our request. It is true that God delights to answer prayer, and we should remember that Jesus encouraged us to ask for things so that our joy would be full. However, our relationship with God needs to consist of more than our expecting Him to preserve us or bail us out from difficulties.

Rather, life is more about bringing glory to God.

Again, that should not stop us from bringing our requests to Him, but as we grow as Christians, we also take on burdens that are on the heart of God, not just our own.

UNDERLYING PRINCIPLES

One of the desires of the apostle Paul was that he would know the "fellowship of His sufferings" (Philippians 3:10). Paul certainly did suffer greatly, but how is this passage worked out in the lives of most of us today who will never be beaten or imprisoned because of our faith? I think the key is in the word, "fellowship." When we are close to someone, we are affected by troubles that they are experiencing because of our love for them. Similarly, the things that sadden Jesus should sadden us if we have fellowship with Him. Sin, rebellion, hate, discrimination, bloodshed, persecution of His people (both Jews and Christians)… these will affect us because we share His sufferings. Our attention turns from the aspects of our own lives to things that trouble Him. In this sense, we share in His sufferings, and our attention is on what matters to Him.

Here are some additional passages that show our purpose is to glorify Him:

- **Psalm 29:1** "Give unto the Lord, O you mighty ones, give unto the Lord glory and strength."

- **Psalm 79:9** "Help us, O God of our salvation, for the glory of Your name."

- **Romans 15:7** "Therefore receive one another, just as Christ also received us, to the glory of God."

- **1 Corinthians 10:31** "Therefore, whether you eat or drink, or whatever you do, do all to the glory of God."

- **2 Corinthians 1:20** "For all the promises of God in Him are Yes, and in Him Amen, to the glory of God through us."

- **Philippians 1:11** "Being filled with the fruits of righteousness which are by Christ Jesus, to the glory and praise of God."

We are to live in such a way that we bring honor to God and please Him

When Samuel was rebuking Saul for his disobedience to the clear command of God, he made a statement that to a Jew living under the law would have been quite astounding. Samuel said, "Has the Lord as great delight in burnt offerings and sacrifices, as in obeying the voice of the Lord? To obey is better than sacrifice…" (1 Samuel 15:22). When he defeated the Amalekites, Saul kept the best of the livestock, ostensibly to sacrifice to the Lord. This certainly sounded very spiritual. What could be more appreciated by God than offerings to Him of the best of the livestock? However, Samuel understood the ways of God. He knew what God really valued, and that was someone who lived their life in obedience to Him and honored Him. This was actually the heart of the law, not the outward observance of its rules.

It is sad to say that we sometimes have trouble obeying a clear instruction from the Lord. Sometimes people will make considerable sacrifices to "make up" for not having been obedient. The Lord has requested something of them that they did not want to do, so they try to compensate by other means. They may sacrifice considerable time and money in other things, hoping that it offsets their disobedience, or perhaps do things to help someone without doing the very thing that they should for that person. But of course, in the eyes of God there is no offset.

The twenty-fourth chapter of Matthew's gospel is generally considered the place to start when studying end time events. Jesus had been sitting on the Mount of Olives with the two sets of brothers, Peter and Andrew, and James and John, answering their questions and providing detailed insight into these future events. At the completion, He asked the question, "Who is a faithful and wise servant whom his master made ruler over his household, to give them food in due season?" He went on to say that the master would make this servant ruler over all his goods. High praise indeed! Then He described what characteristic qualified this servant to be considered faithful and wise, and qualified to receive such a commendation. The answer was, "Blessed is that servant whom his master, when he comes, will find him so doing." (Matthew 24:45-47).

What Jesus was saying is that we are to be found doing precisely what He has asked of us. If this is being a missionary, we need to be a missionary. If it is to be politician, we need to be a politician. If it is being a homemaker, we need to be a homemaker. Of course, in our doing whatever the Lord wants of us, it is a given that we do so in a lifestyle that honors Him, keeping His commands and living righteously.

Sometimes we think that our purpose in life must be something lofty, something prized by the standards of the church or the world, in order to please the Lord. However, that is not what Jesus said. In fact, there are many examples of people in the Bible that God commended who did not do things that would have been regarded as spectacular by most people's standards and yet received commendation for God.

For example, Abraham's servant obeyed his master and found a wife for Abraham's son, Isaac. Isn't carrying out the boss's instructions what a good employee should do?

Ruth cared for her mother-in-law. It was a decision that she made when she left Moab. Isn't caring for close family members a responsibility that we should take?

A man named Obadiah risked his life to hide one hundred prophets of the Lord from the wicked Jezebel in caves and to provide food for them. This is similar to the people who hid Jews during World War II. Did they do it to be praised? No, they did it because they valued human life and cared for defenseless people.

Epaphroditus delivered a gift from the Philippian church to Paul while he was in prison and encouraged him. Did he do it for some reward? Of course not, he did just what the church expected of him, and probably considered it a privilege to help Paul.

These people, and many like them, simply did what they saw was right, having no inkling that their names and deeds would be forever recorded in the Bible and read by millions of people over several centuries, and throughout eternity. We see then that what matters is our faithfulness to what the Lord has called us to do, regardless of how seemingly important or seemingly unimportant that may be.

I think of my wife's grandmother. Outside of her church, family, and some friends she was completely unknown. You will not have heard of her, and you won't find her mentioned on the internet. But she prayed daily, particularly for the church missionaries. Who knows what she accomplished.

Having reverence for God

We are not going to progress very far in our Christian walk without having a heartfelt reverence for God. One of the Ten Commandments is not to take His name in vain, which we could say means that in every way we act and speak we show the utmost respect for Him. We should not be frivolous regarding God, or have a casual attitude to Him or to the Bible, which is the word of God, inspired by the Holy Spirit. Our reverence is demonstrated by:

- our manner

- our respect for things that are precious to Him, such as communion

- living to please Him, not just by our deeds, but in the way we talk and the way we think

- our worship of Him

- our love for the Bible

- our love for His people

- our obedience to His commands.

It is very clear that the saints of both testaments revered God and we must emulate them. To illustrate the importance of reverence, or we could say having the fear of God, let us consider a man named Lot. He lived in the city of Sodom and must have been well respected because he became a city official. He was a successful livestock owner, and the apostle Peter describes him as being a righteous man who was deeply troubled by the rampant sin in the city where he lived (2 Peter 2:7-8). God sent two angels to rescue Lot and his family before the destruction of that city. However, we read that it took considerable persuasion on the part of the angels to get him out so that he did not perish with the rest of the population. Although they pressed him urgently, the angels ultimately had to lead him out by the hand because he did not seem to grasp the perilous situation he was in. Lot even negotiated with them regarding where he should go (Genesis 19:15-22). He just didn't seem to get it.

By contrast, his uncle Abraham was called a friend of God, so much so that before the angels went to Sodom, God said, "Shall I hide from Abraham what I am doing…" The destruction of Sodom would not affect Abraham directly (Genesis 18:17) but God just wanted fellowship with Abraham, like close friends on earth who share the details of their lives. This really is astonishing, to realize the depth of relationship that God desires with people.

Lot was oblivious to the impending disaster, whereas Abraham knew that Sodom would be destroyed before the event took place. So, what was the difference between Lot and Abraham, since both are described as being righteous? The difference is that while Lot was righteous, he was not holy, or to put it another way, the fear of God was not in his life. It is interesting that his name means "veil" or "covering." While he honored God in the way he conducted himself, he did not revere Him as he should. He had become absorbed into the life of the city and probably his personal business interests, and consequently, he was not able to hear from God in this matter.

His spiritual eyes were covered as if he was wearing a veil and his heart was in Sodom.

The essence of holiness is being separate, or different. This certainly does not mean that we become weird, nor does it mean that we should escape to some remote place to live a life without the influence of the corrupt world. That might be separate and different, but it is very unlikely that God would be leading us in that direction. Instead, we have to be obedient and live where the Lord places us. Holiness stems from an attitude of the heart. From the bottom of our heart, we must revere God and hold Him in the highest of respect.

We should not be afraid of God in the sense that He will turn on us, but we should be very afraid of the consequences of disobedience that we can bring upon ourselves. Fear, as in being afraid of something, in contrast to the fear of God, is illustrated in Exodus 20:20 where Moses said to the people, "Do not fear, for God has come to test you, that His fear may be upon you." The statement at first sounds like a contradiction. We are not to fear, so that we will be in fear. This apparent contradiction is explained by understanding the different uses of the word "fear." Moses was saying not to be afraid (fear as we normally use the word, being afraid of something), because God wanted the people to fear the Lord (respect, honor, revere, hold in awe).

It is not sufficient to live a righteous life, even though that is a high standard in itself. We must also live in the fear of the Lord if we wish to have Him teach us His ways. In Malachi 3:16-18, we see the special regard God has for those who walk in the fear of the Lord. He refers to them as being "Mine" and as "My jewels." And He listens to their conversations. They are very special to Him.

We can also consider Isaiah 33:6 where we read that, "The fear of the Lord is His treasure." If God regards something as being His treasure, it is of vital importance that we embrace it if we want to know His ways.

We will limit our spiritual growth if the fear of the Lord is not in our life. We may become like Lot who was righteous, but still lacking an essential ingredient to qualify us to understand His ways.

HOW CAN WE LEARN THE WAYS OF GOD?

How can we learn the ways of God? Such a good question, such an important question. In Psalm 25:4, David asked, "Show me your ways, Oh Lord; teach me Your paths," which shows that understanding the ways of God was something he valued highly. It also shows that the ways and the paths of the Lord are not something we can enter into without the help of the Lord. We need Him to reveal them to us and to help us to walk in them.

The good news is that we can indeed learn His ways. In Isaiah 2:3 we read, "Come, let us go up to the mountain of the Lord, to the house of the God of Jacob; He will teach us His ways, and we shall walk in His paths." So, there is a means whereby we can learn the ways of God. We have to place ourselves in a position where He can teach us. In the days of Isaiah, the presence of God was in the temple on Mount Zion in Jerusalem, and this is what Isaiah was referring to when he spoke of going up to the mountain of the Lord. Fortunately, in our day as Christian people, we do not have to go to the city of Jerusalem to seek the Lord. For us, seeking Him is a matter of our heart.

Learning the ways of God is so important. In Jeremiah 13:23 we read, "Can the Ethiopian change his skin or the leopard his spots? Then may you also do good who are accustomed to do evil." Obviously, the color of our skin is what it is, changed only somewhat by exposure to the sun which causes the skin to darken until that exposure ceases and then it quickly returns to its natural color. And the coat of a leopard always has spots, they never change. So, if there are differences in the standards of righteousness between us and God, differences in how we view things in life, or differences in outlook, these differences have to be resolved in order for us to truly walk with God. Of course, God is holy, His judgments are true and right, so He is not the one who has to make the changes. No, any changes must be made in our thinking and in our behaviors. We have to come into alignment with God. Fortunately, unlike our skin color and the coat of a leopard, we can change our ways because in His death, Jesus paid for our sin so that we can have a transformed heart (Hebrews 8:10).

There are two main avenues whereby God teaches us His ways, and in both cases we are dependent upon His teaching us. They are through the Bible, and through life's experiences. Through these tools, God instructs us. Sometimes the instruction is a revelation that He gives to us. Sometimes, it is something that we learn from events, both good and bad. Sometimes He actually speaks truth into our mind, in a thought or in a sentence. Whatever the avenue, we need His insight to be passed on to us. Without God opening our spiritual eyes and understanding, these avenues will be merely good advice and/or events that occur in our life. However, if our heart is right with Him, we are candidates for His instruction, and the blessings that flow from it.

The Bible

As mentioned earlier, this amazing Book was written with the most precise mathematical patterns that are unequaled in any other literature, proving the inspiration of the Bible as written in its original languages. Consequently, it provides considerable insight into the nature of God, and His ways. In our courtrooms, we continually use DNA and fingerprints to convict or acquit the person accused of a crime. These tools are recognized as conclusive proof because the probability of accuracy is so high. The same is true for the original writings of the Bible, both Old and New Testaments. The probability of the original texts being inspired is so high that we have to conclude that the writings are inspired by the Holy Spirit working through the writers.

Knowing the Bible is inspired is wonderful but unless we learn from it, that truth does not profit us. We must be people who read it, study it, think about it. Further, having understood that the Bible is inspired requires that we obey its teaching. The Bible is truly remarkable. It provides practical instruction for living, and insight into the nature of God. It will teach us about His ways.

We will look at some passages that illustrate His ways, but there are so many passages we cannot examine more than a few in this book.

Revelation 22:11 "He who is unjust, let him be unjust still; he who is filthy, let him be filthy still; he who is righteous, let him be righteous still; he who is holy, let him be holy still." God is perfectly fair. In this verse He is saying that we can select the path for our lives, and He will confirm us in that path. The lesson here is similar to when God brought the plagues upon Egypt. There we read that He hardened Pharaoh's heart, but God was not unfair in doing so because we also read that Pharaoh hardened his own heart toward God. God gave us free will, the ability and right to make our own choices. Of course, we live with the consequences, whether they be good or bad, and the lesson regarding His ways is that He respects our decisions. Therefore, it behooves us to ask Him for wisdom and for His guidance and be willing to be obedient.

I can think of people who came to the Lord and changed their ways, and because of the change in their heart and direction, the Lord enabled them to become very mature Christians. He confirmed them in their newly chosen path. Sadly, I can think of others who were determined to follow an unrighteous path. God showed mercy to them, alerting them to the error of their ways, but because they did not heed the warnings their lives have become more and more unrighteous.

Matthew 3:10 "The axe is laid to the root of the tree." Whatever does this passage teach us about learning the ways of God?" I think it applies to how we view sin. I once had a tree that I chopped down, but it continued to sprout new prospective trees from its very roots. I tried mowing them along with the grass, but I continued to have these little trees springing up in my yard. It was not until I removed the roots that I ceased to have these small trees. When the very root of a tree is chopped out, there is no possibility for the tree to sprout new "trees." Similarly, when dealing with sin in our lives it is important that we do not leave "roots." Judas Iscariot teaches us this lesson. He was one of the inner circle of twelve men who were privileged to receive Jesus' explanations of His parables, hear all of His teaching, observe His lifestyle every day, and see the miracles that He performed. And yet Judas failed terribly. Why? Because he was a thief, and he never fully dealt with his love of money. It is possible that he reduced the size of that "tree" but he did not take out the roots. We have to truly desire to be free from sin, not accommodating it.

Psalm 23:1 "The Lord is my shepherd..." David was given considerable revelation regarding the ways of God, and in this psalm he likens his relationship to God as being like that of a shepherd with his sheep. David himself was a shepherd in his youth and knew what it took to care for his flock. He saw that God took care of him in a similar manner. He saw also that just as sheep need to have a shepherd, he also needed one. Also, he understood the very personal relationship between sheep and shepherd, between God and himself. Understanding God's ways entails understanding Him as a shepherd and allowing Him to "shepherd" our lives.

Luke 1:53 "He has filled the hungry with good things, and the rich He has sent away empty." God gives His good things to those who want them. A person who has a casual attitude toward the things of God will receive very little. God looks for people who truly desire to know Him and are willing to invest their time and efforts in seeking Him, and to live the kind of life that is pleasing to Him.

Those who know that there is so much more to learn and experience are "hungry" and He rewards them for it. However, those who think they are "rich" and don't expend much effort to know God receive little from Him.

1 Peter 1:16 "Because it is written, be holy for I am holy." Peter is quoting from several passages in Leviticus such as 19:2. God is holy, meaning that He is set apart, different in the very best sense, and He requires us to be holy too. This is not the standard that the Pharisees adopted in Jesus' day. Theirs was one of conformance to rules, but the Bible is speaking of being transformed within so that we are like Him, not just in our behavior, not just in how we speak, but also in how we think. It is an enormously high standard, and we can only achieve it with His enabling. But that is the standard that we must ask Him to accomplish in us.

I am reminded of a vision that a man had. He saw himself climbing a mountain, and periodically he came to a beautiful valley. As he progressed up the mountain the valleys became more and more beautiful. They were occupied by Christians who were very happy, and in each one they thought that they had arrived at the ultimate blessing of God. However, each time he thought of stopping in a valley, the Lord told him to continue to climb. Soon the climbing was very difficult and the path barely discernible, but presently he reached the top of the mountain. Now think about a mountain...is there a valley at the top? No, there is the peak. So, in the vision, when the man reached the top there was no beautiful valley. However, the Lord Himself came to the man. How much better than any valley, no matter how beautiful that valley might be! The application for us is that we should not stop at some level in our Christian walk and experience, no matter how pleasant it is. Instead, we must continually press onward, the Lord helping us through difficult times. The reward is not just a blessing but the Lord Himself. Priceless!

God teaching us through life's experiences

When we look at the life of Jesus, there is an interesting, even curious aspect pertaining to His developing into His ministry. At the age of twelve, He had traveled to Jerusalem for the feast of Passover, and after about a day's travel on their journey home, his parents realized that Jesus was not among their company. Returning to Jerusalem to locate Him, they found Him in the temple, conversing with the teachers. In Luke 2:47 we read that, "All who heard Him were astonished at His answers." Even at twelve, Jesus must have had an amazing command of the scriptures and understanding of the principles behind them.

To our way of thinking, Jesus was already equipped for ministry at the age of twelve and we would have arranged for Him to speak in churches and conferences across the county. Even at such a young age, He was already a sensation. However, it would be another eighteen years before the Father saw fit to launch Jesus into a public ministry. If He was so sharp at twelve, why did He have to wait all that additional time until He was thirty? After all, He was the perfect Son of God. The reasons are not explained in the Bible but there are some passages that provide insight.

In Hebrews 5:8 we read of Jesus, "Though He was a son, yet He learned obedience by the things that He suffered." This cannot be referring to the time of His crucifixion because His obedience was proved in His accepting the will of the Father that day. He didn't learn to be obedient on that day. Neither can it refer to the three-and-one-half years of His ministry because His obedience in those years was crucial to success. Again, that was not His time of learning. It has to be referring to the years beforehand, those first thirty years of His life, and certain difficulties, even suffering in some manner, that were an essential part of His preparation.

In Isaiah 49:2 we read, "…and he made me a polished shaft…" This is an illustration taken from the production of arrows. The shafts were made from branches of trees, and all the imperfections and little bumps would have to be polished away for that arrow to be fit for use. Without a perfectly straight, smooth shaft, the arrow would veer off course and miss its intended target. As we know, Jesus was the Son of God, but besides being divine, He was also human. As the Son of God, He was born without the sin nature that we have and He never sinned. However, before being launched into His ministry, all those aspects of humanity that could potentially deflect Him had to be addressed. So, Jesus had to suffer through various trials in order that He would be a polished shaft and fly true in His ministry to achieve the purpose for His life, the cross. Had He not learned obedience and been polished, He might have been deflected by the enormity of what He was to pass through when He took upon Himself the sins of the world.

Obedience to the will of the Father must have been one of the most important human aspects to address, probably the most important of all. How did Jesus learn obedience? By the things that He suffered. We are not told what these things were, just that they were in His life.

If it was necessary for the Father to teach Jesus obedience through the difficulties that He experienced, it must be necessary for us as well. Trials and difficulties prove out what we really believe and bring to the surface what is in our heart when we respond to a given situation. For example, we can quote the scripture verse, "All things work together for good for those who love God..." (Romans 8:28), but what do we really believe when things go wrong. Through no fault of our own, we lose our job, lose our retirement funds, have a death of a loved one, suffer through a church problem, suffer betrayal... the list of possibilities is very long. How do we react?

Some people are like the soil that was shallow in the Parable of the Sower, and having begun their Christian walk well, they do not continue and falter. Perhaps an unrealized expectation causes them to become disillusioned and their fire goes out. If we are to grow closer to God, we cannot be like that soil. We must be like the good soil that brought forth a crop. The good soil is described as those who, "hear the word and understand it." To "hear and understand" the word we must have a receptive heart, one that takes in the Word of God and applies it.

Our relationship with God and our understanding of His nature cannot be based on the circumstances of our life. Initially as a young Christian, it may be based on what we read in the Bible and on other people's experiences, but in time, we have to know God and His truth for ourselves. We cannot progress very far on other people's coattails.

SOME THINGS THAT GOD VALUES

If we want to learn the ways of God, and for His ways to become our ways too, we need to consider what God regards as being important and the things that He values. We must become people who love the things that He loves. As we read the Bible, and look around us at creation and life itself, there are certain things that stand out as being of significant importance to God. Things such as certain qualities like righteousness and kindness are important to Him because that is how He is too. Obviously, we cannot examine many of the things that He values as that would entail several volumes, but we will look at a few that might not be as obvious.

The children of Israel, the Jews

It is amazing how God has regard for human beings. We are created beings, prone to sin and to going our own way, and yet He loves us very dearly. That love was so great that Jesus humbled Himself and became a man like us. Forever He is identified with us. He has a body which will no doubt be like the glorified bodies that we will ultimately receive. And if that was not enough, He paid for our reconciliation to God with His own suffering and blood.

There are some people who, because of their character and love for God, are in turn particularly special in the eyes of God. It is not that He is unfair to anyone, but there are some who have earned a special place with Him. For example, Daniel was considered, "greatly beloved," John was "the disciple whom Jesus loved," God spoke with Moses "face to face," Noah "found grace in the eyes of the Lord," and God describes those who feared the Lord (in Malachi 3:16-18) as His jewels. Another person was Abraham, who God referred to as His friend, and God made a covenant with Abraham, part of which entailed his descendants being a chosen people who would possess the land where Abraham dwelt, the land of Israel.

The children of Israel have inherited God's blessing. God called the descendants of Abraham, through Isaac and Jacob, to be a chosen people to Himself. God made a covenant with Abraham regarding his descendants (Genesis 12:1-3) and he confirmed it with his son Isaac (Genesis 26:3-4), and reaffirmed it with Isaac's son, Jacob (Genesis 28:14-15). This is the reason why it is common for God to be referred to as the God of Abraham, Isaac, and Jacob. Jacob, whose name God changed to Israel, had twelve sons who became the heads of the tribes, and they and their descendants are the children of Israel.

It is important that we understand that God's covenant with Abraham cannot be broken, and that forever the Jewish people are chosen as a special treasure to Him, in spite of times when they have turned away from following God. Covenants are very strong, binding agreements. To signify the strength of their covenant, the two parties would cut an animal or animals in two and walk between their bodies. Cutting the animals signified the depth of the oath. In Genesis chapter 15, we read that Abraham prepared the animals, and we also read that God made a covenant with him (Genesis 15:18). The covenant was between God and Abraham, but who sealed that covenant?

I believe that God understood the frailty of human nature and that Abraham's descendants would fail to wholeheartedly follow Him. So, while the covenant was made between God and Abraham, it was sealed by the Father and the Son. In Genesis 15:17, we find that the parties who passed between the animal pieces were a smoking oven and a burning torch. The Father is described as being a consuming fire (Hebrews 12:29) and the Son is the light of the world (John 8:12). In symbolic form, the covenant was sealed by the Father and the Son, and therefore it can never be broken. In spite of how the Jews have at times rejected God, the covenant still stands. And at the time He sees fit, God will cause them to recognize Jesus as their Messiah and bring them into great blessing, although the path to this revelation will be exceedingly difficult for them.

I think David understood that the covenant between God and Israel would stand forever and could not be replaced. In his conversation with God in 2 Samuel 7:23-24 he said, "Who is like Your people, like Israel, the one nation on earth whom God went to redeem for Himself… You have made Your people Israel Your very own people forever."

This truth is confirmed in other passages of the Bible. In a statement to the Jews, Isaiah 54:10 says, "My kindness shall not depart from you, nor shall my covenant of peace be removed." Jeremiah 33:25 says, "If my covenant is not with day and night, and if I have not appointed the ordinances of heaven and earth, then I will cast away the descendants of

Jacob..." And Ezekiel 16:8 says, "Yes, I swore an oath to you and entered into a covenant with you, and you became Mine." The same theme is echoed by the apostle Paul who wrote, "Has God cast away His people? Certainly not! God has not cast away His people... (Romans 11:1-2). God keeps His promises, and the children of Israel are a special people to Him. Consequently, we also need to regard them as special in the eyes of God.

The Land of Israel

God told Abraham to walk through the land of Canaan which He had led him into, and He told him the boundaries of that land which would one day become the possession of his descendants. Those boundaries were first expressed as the territories held by other nations at that time, and later stated in geographical terms. (Genesis 15:18-21, Exodus 23:28-31). This was an amazing promise. God told a man that his descendants would possess a portion of the earth, and this promise was given before Abraham had any children!

How does God view this particular area that He designated to the children of Israel? In Joel 3:2 we sense His anger that the land has been divided and refers to it as *His* land. In fact, today the nation of Israel does not extend fully to the borders that God promised and yet world leaders talk of "partitioning" or dividing it so that Israel's portion becomes even smaller, not larger. This cannot be pleasing to God.

While it is true that God loves the land of Israel, we also find that the city of Jerusalem holds a special place in His heart. In 2 Chronicles 6:6 we read, "Yet I have chosen Jerusalem, that My name may be there." Also, we are told that we will prosper if we have a love for Jerusalem (Psalm 122:6), no doubt because God so loves that city. If we are to walk in the ways of God, we also need to have a love for Jerusalem, and the nation and land of Israel.

The Sabbath day

The fourth of the Ten Commandments (Exodus 20:8-11) says, "Remember the Sabbath, to keep it holy." Every seventh day we are to do no work. The command included employees and working animals, all of whom were to take a day of rest. This is in recognition of how God rested on the seventh day after creation, and the command concludes with the words, "Therefore the Lord blessed the Sabbath day and hallowed it."

What can we draw from the words of this commandment?

Firstly, we should note that it is a command from God to us. Therefore, it must not be taken lightly. It is not a suggestion, an option, or a good idea. It is a command and needs to be obeyed.

Secondly, it is something important to God. He instructed us to keep it holy, He blessed it, and hallowed it. When something is hallowed it is consecrated, revered, and honored. There are many passages in the Bible that confirm the importance of the Sabbath to God. For example:

- **Exodus 31:14** "Everyone who profanes it (the Sabbath) shall be put to death."

- **Isaiah 56:2** "Blessed is the man who does this (keeps justice and righteousness), who keeps from defiling the Sabbath…"

- **Ezekiel 20:20** "Hallow My Sabbaths and they will be a sign between Me and you, that you may know that I am the Lord your God."

Therefore, if for no other reason than to please our wonderful heavenly Father, we need to have one day each week that is set aside to honor Him and to rest.

Thirdly, it is for our benefit. We all need rest periodically, and we ignore taking times for rest to our own detriment. Again, there are many passages in the Bible that support this, such as:

- **Exodus 16:13-26** The Lord provided manna for the people to eat, but every sixth day they were to gather twice as much as normal because there would be no manna on the seventh day so that they could have a day of rest. Interestingly, if they gathered extra during the first five days it did not keep until the following day but became moldy. This was a miraculous provision, and it was intended to teach us that we can accomplish more in six days with a day of rest than we can in seven days with no rest. In the French Revolution, the leaders introduced a ten day work week to increase productivity, and later the Soviets experimented with five and six day work weeks. Both governments had to revert to a seven day week because productivity declined rather than improved. It is how God made us, requiring a day of rest in each week.

- In **Isaiah 56:4-5**, God lists special promises to eunuchs who "Keep My Sabbaths and choose what pleases Me." Keeping the Sabbath was specifically mentioned by God as necessary to receive the promises.

- **Mark 2:27** Jesus plainly stated that, "The Sabbath was made for man, not man for the Sabbath." In so saying, He was pointing out that the reason for the day of rest is for our benefit rather than a rule that we keep.

The Sabbath day was a Saturday in Jesus' time, and still is in Israel today. However, the early church changed their day of worship to Sunday because that was the day of the week when Jesus rose from the dead. For most Christian people today, their day of rest will also be a Sunday. Does this mean that they have selected the wrong day? I do not believe so. While Sunday is the most convenient day for most of us, some people must work on Sundays, often performing essential services such as in the medical field. The principle is that we rest on one day each week.

We understand then that having one day of rest each week is important. By so doing, we honor God and benefit ourselves by being refreshed, which enables us to be more productive in the other six days. I found this to be true during the years when I worked in a manufacturing company. I looked forward to Fridays because the weekend followed, but my second-favorite day of the week was Monday because I was refreshed by my day of rest and my energy renewed. It was always a very productive day.

Care for people

In Isaiah chapter 58, God makes some wonderful promises to those who are considerate toward other people in need. Among them are promises to guide us continually, for our darkness to be as bright as the middle of the day, and our life to be like a watered garden. Wonderful indeed! What then, are the qualifications for receiving these promises? They relate to how we treat others.

I heard of a lady who was privileged to go to heaven and while there she saw that angels were recording the actions of people on earth. She was surprised that what we would consider to be small and trivial things, such as a kind word and a smile, were being recorded. If the angels are recording them, they must be important in the eyes of God.

In the same chapter in Isaiah, we read how the people had a show of piety but neglected the things that were most important to God. The people brought sacrifices and engaged in spiritual activities such as fasting, all of which is excellent, but they must be accompanied by a life that pleases Him. It is not what we do but what we really are, from our heart, that counts. If the heart is right, what we do will normally be right as well.

In a number of places in the Bible, God makes it clear that it is our heart that He looks at, not our performing religious acts. For example, when the Pharisees criticized Jesus' disciples for not washing their hands before eating, Jesus told them that it was not what goes into our mouth that defiles us but what comes of it, referring to how we talk (Matthew 5:11). And even though the people in the days of Malachi made offerings to the Lord and wept over the altar, God did not accept their offering because they had been dealing treacherously with their wives (Malachi 2:13-15). It is only logical that our living righteous lives would matter to a righteous God more than a show of religious acts.

Throughout the Bible, we find God addressing our need to care for others. One of the commands in the law was, "You shall not afflict any widow or fatherless child" (Exodus 22:22). In those days, there were no government assistance programs to help people with needs and consequently, life was hard for a widow or a fatherless child. So, God commanded that they be treated with care.

The law contained provision for strangers, widows, and fatherless children to find food by gleaning what was overlooked by the harvesters (Deuteronomy 24:20-21). Moreover, the harvesters were instructed to intentionally overlook some of the produce. The law commanded them to not to go over their harvest a second time, nor were they to glean the corners of their fields, but instead leave that grain for those who had no other means of feeding themselves. In the wisdom of God, the dignity of these vulnerable people was being preserved because they had to work for their living. The law required them to work, not beg, and also the temptation to steal was reduced because food was available. The law of God provided a means for them to earn their living and preserve their dignity. Wise indeed! And the property owners were blessed by keeping the instruction of the law of God by showing kindness to poor and vulnerable people.

Worship

Throughout the Bible, we find people worshiping God. Unfortunately, we also find people worshiping idols, the sun, the moon, and other objects. Nebuchadnezzar erected a statue, and under penalty of death, commanded that the people worship it. It is clear that Satan desires to be worshiped and to be considered like God, as evidenced in the temptations of Jesus where he offered the kingdoms of the world to Jesus if He would worship him. We are designed with a need to worship, whether as a conscious act or not. The question is, what or who will be the object of our worship?

This brings us to the matter of idolatry, a sin which led to Jerusalem being destroyed and the Jews being taken into captivity by the Babylonians. Today, idolatry as practiced at that time in Jerusalem is not widespread in the western world, although many people have idols and items associated with witchcraft in their homes as decorations or charms. Unfortunately, they are unaware that there are demons behind the idols, and by having an idol or charm, they are inviting a demon into their home and to have an influence in their life. These images are not cute decorations – they are an abomination to God, and they endanger the spiritual life of those in the home.

Why does God hate idols? One reason is that they are false gods, whereas He is the one true God and only He should be honored. It is such an affront to Him to replace Him with some other object of our heart's affection. Another reason is the harm that we bring to ourselves through any form of idolatry. God loves us and does not want us under the influence of an evil spirit.

God desires our worship, and this is clear in many, many passages of the Bible. Even in the Ten Commandments, God said that we are to have no god before Him. Does this mean that God has such an inferiority complex that He needs to be worshiped to build up His ego? Such a notion is entirely contradictory to the revelation of God in the Bible and to the experience of millions of people. So why is being worshiped so important to Him? I think there are two reasons.

One reason is that it is a choice that we make. There is nothing that we can give to God that He has need of, nor that He does not already have access to. He doesn't need a house, a car, or any material item. He doesn't need our money, although He does want us to tithe our income so that His work on earth is funded and so that we can come under His blessing because the tithe is holy to Him. So, what do we have to offer? Just worship and gratitude.

When creating us, God gave us a free will, the ability to make choices and decisions as we please. The risk with this is that we can make bad choices, and I am sure that everyone can think of a time when they made a bad choice. Some people have made choices that are actually downright evil, resulting in wars, crime, and harm to others. However, there is a great benefit associated with having free will, namely that we can choose to love and worship God. It is similar to a child expressing love and affection to a parent just because they want to. This is so rewarding to the parent, who loves their child and has put so much into caring for him or her. Likewise, God loves us and has done more that we can fully understand to care for us, even offering eternal life to us. So, being made in the image of God, when we express thankfulness and honor Him, loving Him in recognition of His unspeakable majesty, and worshiping Him, it makes His efforts for us worthwhile. I don't think God actually needs anything, but our free will worship is what He deserves. It is the one thing that we can give that He cannot otherwise obtain.

The second reason is that worshiping God is a benefit to us. He is so unselfish, so immeasurably kind and generous, that in giving to Him we receive blessings from Him. The most precious experiences of His presence that I have known have come in times when I was worshiping Him, either alone or with others. Inevitably, when we worship and praise Him, the Holy Spirit comes to us, bringing that beautiful sense of the presence of God. There is nothing like it, nothing to compare to it.

In the Bible, there are several references to God being worshiped by the citizens of heaven, some angels and some people. From these passages, we obtain insight as to why God is worshiped. It is not only because worship is all we have to offer Him, or because of the blessing that we receive in return. It is because of who He is.

In Revelation 4:8-11 and Revelation 5:8-14, the apostle John describes what he saw of the worship of God by those who are around the throne and in close proximity to Him. They are in a position to see just how God is, and the result is that they worship Him. They describe Him as holy, which is a difficult word for us to understand because we have no proper comparison on earth. The basic meaning of "holy" has to do with being separate, but when it comes to describing God, it is a word that designates Him as being transcendentally separate, so far above everything and everyone else. They also speak of His being worthy of worship, and that all honor belongs to Him and to Jesus, the Lamb of God.

As these ones around the throne see and consider God, they are quite overcome by His majesty. They fall down before Him and worship Him, and this is something that they never tire of doing! Why do they not tire? It is because of who God is. Being in close contact with Him is the most wonderful thing one can experience, and when we are close to Him, all we want to do is worship Him. I have found that in times when His presence is particularly strong, my thoughts don't waver, and my attention is fixed on Him. How much more must be this experience around the throne of God.

Prayers

God loves our prayers. In Revelation chapter five, we have the awesome account of the scroll being handed by the Father to Jesus, the Lamb of God. Jesus was the only One in heaven or earth who was worthy to open that scroll. Appropriately in verse eight, when Jesus takes the scroll, the four living creatures and the twenty-four elders who are around the throne of God, fall down and worship the Lamb. The passage then tells us that they each held two things. One was a harp, possibly as an instrument of worship. The second was a golden bowl. And what was inside the bowls? The prayers of the saints.

Similarly, in chapter eight we have the account of the opening of the seventh seal, an occasion that was so dramatic that there was silence in heaven for about a half an hour, probably in anticipation of the awesome judgments that were to follow. In verses three and four, we read about an angel who has a golden censor with which to bring an offering of a sweet fragrance to God. But there is something else that the angel includes in this offering – the prayers of the saints. "The smoke of the incense, with the prayers of the saints, ascended before God from the angel's hand."

It is astounding how God values our prayers. We look at prayer as communicating requests and thanks to God, and to simply talking to Him about the many and varied things of our life. To us, prayers are our communication with God as opposed to our communication with people, and particularly in the case of our requests, there is an aspect of benefit to us that results from praying. However, it would seem that God has a different perspective. He views prayers as something of benefit to Him. God values our prayers so highly that they are like incense, a lovely fragrance that He can enjoy.

We might well wonder how it is that our ineloquent words, our inadequate way of saying what is on our mind, our wandering thoughts…how all these imperfections could still be so valued by Almighty God. It brings to mind one of the qualities that God declared about Himself to Moses in Exodus 34:6, that of being gracious. To be gracious means *to bend or stoop in kindness to an inferior,* and most definitely that describes God's behavior toward us.

We view prayer from our own perspective, but if we are to understand prayer, we must also see it from God's perspective. We see the benefit to us when we ask God to move and change situations and circumstances. However, God sees prayer as an offering to Him. Like worship, we pray from our own choice. It is not something that God extracts from us, but something that we bring from our own free will out of love, faith, humility, and respect. I believe that is why prayer is so valued by God.

There was an occasion when the Lord spoke to my wife regarding prayer. He said, "If you understood prayer, you would pray more and see My power." The statement has challenged us ever since. I think "pray more and see My power" is not too hard to understand, but what does He mean when He says we need to "understand" prayer? I believe part of the answer lies in the revelation of the importance God places on the prayers of the saints, how He regards them as so precious that they are collected in golden bowls and are a sweet fragrance to Him. I suspect that there is more for me to learn, and that statement continues to challenge me to seek Him for further insight.

EXAMPLES

There are many examples in the Bible of situations where the ways of God run counter-intuitive to our way of thinking. We should not think that doing things that are counter-intuitive means that we are more spiritually mature because that is not the case. God gave us a mind and expects us to use it, and most of our guidance should be common sense. However, there are occasions when His way is different from how we would have thought or acted. We will consider some of these.

Jeroboam's Young Son

In 1 Kings 14:1-18, there is a story about King Jeroboam and one of his sons. Jeroboam had been an officer under King Solomon, and a prophet named Ahijah met him and told him that the kingdom would be divided and he would become ruler over the ten of the tribes of the northern kingdom. This took place under Solomon's successor, Rehoboam. Ahijah also gave Jeroboam a wonderful prophecy, not unlike the one given to David. The promise was that God would be with him and would give him an enduring house. In other words, his descendants would continue on his throne. However, there was a condition which we read in 1 Kings 11:38. The condition was that Jeroboam must, "Walk in My ways, and do what is right in My sight, and keep My statutes and commandments." This Jeroboam did not do, and instead of trusting God to fulfill His promise, he introduced idolatry into his kingdom and led his people astray, fearing that they would desert him because the temple was located in the southern kingdom. When reading about other kings who succeeded him, the Bible often says that they "Walked in the ways of Jeroboam who made Israel to sin." He became a standard for unrighteousness in the kingdom, not something to be emulated.

Jeroboam had several sons, one of whom was still a boy. Jeroboam must have loved the boy because when he became very sick, Jeroboam sent his wife to Ahijah to inquire of the Lord as to the fate of his young son. How do you think we would have reacted if the lady had come to us? It is highly likely that we would have prayed earnestly for the boy's recovery. We would have been sympathetic because not only was he still very young, but also because he was recognized as being a really good boy.

However, under the leading of the Holy Spirit, what did Ahijah do? His approach was very different. He proceeded to tell the lady that God had seen how Jeroboam failed to walk in His ways and had turned away from Him, and that He will bring disaster on Jeroboam, cutting off all his descendants. Moreover, some of them would die grisly deaths. Then Ahijah addressed the state of the boy, and said that he would die from his illness, "…because in him there is found something good toward the Lord God" (1 Kings 14:13). Doesn't that sound wrong to us, that the boy would die because he had a heart for God, because he was not evil like his father? Shouldn't his good nature be grounds for God to preserve him? Certainly it sounds wrong, but not when we understand the merciful ways of God.

Ahijah said that the people would mourn for the boy and that he would receive a proper burial, unlike the rest of Jeroboam's sons. How do you think the people would have reacted when the boy died? He must have been popular and of good character, and they might say, "Why did he have to die? He was such a good boy, why didn't God heal him?" That is our human logic. But God was looking to the future.

The people had no knowledge regarding the conversation between Ahijah and Jeroboam's wife, no knowledge of the judgment that God decreed upon the house of Jeroboam, so their reaction may well have been like we described above, questioning the character of God because a good person died young. However, God was acting in kindness toward the boy by taking him so that he did not suffer the death and degradation that would come upon his brothers. It was in the mercy and goodness of God that he died. This is why it is so important that we are fully grounded in an understanding of the nature and character of God. The correct position for the people would have been to realize that there must be some good reason that was not apparent, and not to question God's character.

We don't always understand why some things happen and sometimes the events are very painful to us. But God is good. Always. We have only limited insight, but He is looking at longer-term objectives.

As an aside, please do not assume that if a couple suffers the loss of a child it is because of their sin and that God will soon judge them for it. There are many possible reasons why a certain event takes place, and we may never fully understand.

Elijah and Elisha

Elijah was a mighty prophet and holds such a place of honor that he was with Moses on the Mount of Transfiguration, talking to Jesus. Elisha was his successor, and also a mighty prophet. In fact, he asked for a double portion of the anointing upon Elijah...and he received it.

In many ways, their lives were similar as they brought the word of the Lord to the northern kingdom of Israel in a time when that kingdom had turned its back on God instead of following Him. Even their departures from this world were associated with supernatural occurrences. Elijah actually did not die. He was taken up to heaven in a chariot of fire (2 Kings 2:11). What an amazing event!

Because of his own stature as a prophet, we might expect that Elisha would have some similar, dramatic departure. However, in 2 Kings 13:14 we read that Elisha contracted an illness and would die from it. Why would God take Elijah in a chariot of fire while Elisha had to endure a sickness that would ultimately take his life? The answer is not obvious to us, and the Bible provides no explanation.

In spite of Elisha's death being unspectacular, an astonishing event would take place some time later. A party of men were burying a man when they sighted a band of raiders from Moab. Not having time to complete the burial, they laid the body in the tomb of Elisha, which must have been nearby. When the dead man's body touched the bones of Elisha, he suddenly came back to life! (2 Kings 13:20-21). Without question, this was a sign that God had regard for this prophet, but the question is, why would God demonstrate His endorsement of Elisha in this manner? Why not take him in a chariot like Elijah, or at least spare him an illness that probably caused his life to ebb away over some period of time? We do not know the answers to these questions. We have to be content in our knowledge of the wisdom and goodness of God, knowing that in some way, His plans and treatment of the two prophets were perfect.

The One Who Obeys the Lord but Walks in Darkness

When we read Isaiah 50:10, we find a statement that seems backwards to us. The passage says, "Who among you fears the Lord? Who obeys the voice of His servant? Who walks in darkness and has no light? Let him trust in the name of the Lord and rely upon his God." We might well wonder, how is it that someone can fear God and be obedient to Him but have to walk in darkness with no light? It just seems all wrong. Fearing God and being obedient to Him should be the keys to having clarity in our direction, not darkness.

Yet anyone who has been a committed Christian for some years knows that this experience actually happens. There are times when God seems so distant and guidance so vague, even though we are living righteously, serving Him and trusting in Him.

There are examples in the Bible, particularly in the psalms. Many of the psalms provide insight into the experiences of the writers, their joys and sorrows, triumphs and trials. An example of walking in dark times is found in Psalm 13 where David wrote, "How long, O Lord? Will You forget me forever? How long will You hide your face from me?" We know that David is someone who God considered to be "a man after My own heart," so how could it be that David would write like this? He was obviously experiencing a time when God seemed so distant that it felt like He had forgotten him.

As he continues in the psalm, David's anguish over his situation is very clear. He says, "How long will my enemy be exalted over me?" He prays, "Enlighten my eyes lest I sleep the sleep of death." It was certainly a tough time, and God seemed to have deserted him.

The psalm does not reveal any details of how David's trial progressed or ended. However, in the last verse he wrote, "I will sing to the Lord, because He has dealt bountifully with me." Given that these words are in the same psalm, it is very possible that at the time he wrote them he was still in the midst of his dark time. David may have been drawing from experience and from his knowledge of God and referring to how God had helped him in the past, which provided a basis for faith for his future. It is certainly very clear that in his lifetime, David trusted in God. This dark experience did not deflect his trust; instead, it caused him to seek after the Lord and to pray to Him.

It is to our benefit that we experience these times of difficulty and darkness, provided we keep pressing on. When we do, we find David's words about the Lord dealing bountifully with us to be true, even when there is a considerable time lapse before He brings us out. We can see only as far as our minds take us, but God sees all the way to the end. He knows the end of a matter from its beginning (Isaiah 46:10). I am very sure that if we could ask David today how he feels about the experience, he would express profound thanks to God for blessing him, and acknowledge that the trial was the only way for God to bring him into a more mature place in his walk. God is always good.

Kadesh Barnea

In Numbers 13 and 14, we read about the failure to enter the Promised Land. Having traveled from Egypt through the desert, the Israelites came to Kadesh Barnea. They were poised to enter into what God had promised. It had taken two years to reach this point, not because of the great distance but because they had camped at various places such as Mount Sinai where they received the Ten Commandments. God was teaching the people and giving them the laws that they were to follow in order to be a holy people and have His continued blessing upon them.

Israel sent twelve spies into the land, and while they all acknowledged that the land was good and produced wonderful crops, ten of the spies so discouraged the people that they wept because, "God had brought them to this land to die by the sword," and even considered appointing a new leader to take them back to Egypt. As a result, God said that those people over the age of twenty would die in the wilderness, and the people wandered for another thirty-eight years until this had been accomplished.

The next morning, the people had a change of heart and decided to go into the Promised Land. They even acknowledged that they had sinned the previous day. How would we view this? Most likely, we would be thrilled that the people had realized their error, repented of their sin, and were now ready to do the right thing. Often in the lives of people today, God is pleased with a change of heart and would enable them to have a second opportunity to be successful. But that is not how God saw it on this occasion because in His wisdom, He knew that the people would fail again.

The Bible provides understanding for us as to why God did not allow that generation to enter the land. In Numbers 14:20-23, God pardoned the people, but we must realize that there are inevitably consequences for our actions. When our actions are wise and righteous, we are blessed as a result, but when they are unwise or rebellious, we usually have to pay a price. So, although God forgave the people, He would not allow that generation to enter the land. His reasons were:

- They had seen His glory and the signs that He performed in Egypt to deliver them.

- They had also seen His glory and signs in the wilderness.

- They had tested Him ten times.

- They did not heed His voice.

When we consider that the people had tested God so many times before Kadesh Barnea, it is little wonder that they failed to obey God and proceed into the land. If we are consistently disobedient, ungrateful, and compromising of God's standards, how would we expect to succeed when it really matters? We might look at God's refusal as a harsh judgment but in reality, it was a great kindness because they would have failed in other situations within the territory of the Promised Land where failure would be catastrophic.

Therefore, considering the ways of God, we have to see His wisdom and far-sightedness. While we would be enamored with the repentance of the people and their change of heart to enter the land, God knew that they were certain to fail. His judgment on the adults over twenty was really a demonstration of His kindness to the whole nation so that He could bring the nation into the Promised Land at a time when they would succeed, and at the same time fulfill His promise to Abraham, Isaac, and Jacob. The ways of God are right. We must be grounded in a proper understanding of His character.

Our Own Lives

In our own lives too, we can often see times when God allowed certain things to happen so that some important purpose could be brought about. I can think of several men that I have known who committed crimes which led to their receiving prison sentences. That is not something that we wish upon another person, as criminal behavior is not exactly praiseworthy and losing one's freedom in a prison sentence is a heavy burden to bear. However, I believe nothing in our lives is wasted if we walk with the Lord, and He turned these terrible situations into something good and productive. All the men that I am thinking of turned their lives to God while serving their sentence, and today would look upon their confinement as a hardship that was necessary for them, and actually a blessing in disguise.

There are people who have a past that involved drug and alcohol abuse, and God leads some of them into a ministry to help others with the same problems. Some people have great struggles in their marriage, and the lessons that they learn become the means to help others in their own marriage difficulties. Sometimes we endure a really hard experience such as losing a business or being fired from our job without good cause, but God then opens another door that we would not have considered had the hardship not changed our course.

I have many examples in my own life. The one that particularly stands out is the five years when my mother was married to my stepfather. It was a terrible, violent time and it left me very damaged. In the end, my mother and I had to run for our lives to the safety of a nearby friend's house, waking them in the night to ask if we could come inside for protection. I was so deeply affected by the time with my stepfather that my hands shook even several years afterward. My life was ruled by fear. However, when the Lord came into my life, He began a healing work and although it took some time, it was a complete work. Those five years were the worst of my life, and I could have asked, "Why did I have to go through this? I was not deserving of such treatment. Why couldn't God have spared me; I was just an innocent boy?" And as if that was enough, not having my stepfather's financial support after we left him meant that my mother and I had to live very economically. I don't think we were poor, but it was a few years before we could afford things like a television.

Today as I look back on those years, I am thankful for them. I have even truly thanked God for my stepfather, and I really do mean it. You see, little did I know that as an adult, God would lead me and my wife into a ministry of counseling, and the experiences of my childhood would enable me to relate to people who had also suffered from a difficult experience. I know how fear affects us, I know what it is to live in danger, and perhaps most importantly, I know the path to healing and being made whole. The worst time of my life became the most productive time of my life. When we walk with the Lord, Romans 8:28 is true. "And we know that all things work together for good to those who love God, to those who are called according to His purpose."

My wife has a good example too. She had experienced several years with a frightening undiagnosed, and at times misdiagnosed, heart condition, which eventually proved to be an issue with the electrical aspects of her heart. One day the Lord gave her a vision. She saw herself entering a tunnel at the base of a mountain. She could not see where she was going but had to just follow the tunnel. Because the tunnel was dark, she had to feel the sides with her hands to know the direction that it led. There was no light to provide guidance for her. Presently, there was a glimmer of light ahead and soon she emerged from the tunnel onto the side of the mountain. To her surprise, she could see the entrance to the tunnel far below her, and realized that without her knowing, she had been climbing during her time in the tunnel. This is what God does for us in dark times. He is providing a way for us to advance in our Christian walk. We might not realize it at the time, but tunnel experiences are often a short-cut for us so we can spiritually advance faster.

WHY WAS MOSES DIFFERENT?

Although His ways are higher than our ways (Isaiah 55:9), and His ways are often unclear to us (Romans 11:33), we are told that God will teach us His ways (Isaiah 2:3, Micah 4:2). These statements appear to be contradictory but on closer examination, the statements speak to different things. The fact that God's ways are higher than ours does not preclude us from learning. It simply points out that there is a considerable difference. And the fact that His ways are unclear at times is pointing out that by our own efforts we will not learn His ways. We are not able to learn them unaided. Psalm 25:12 provides us with a key. It says, "Who is the man that fears the Lord? Him shall He teach in the way that He chooses." If we want to be wise, if we want to have understanding, and if we want God to teach us His ways, we must have the fear of the Lord in our lives.

However, the verses in Isaiah and Micah give us hope that we can indeed learn the ways of God. In both verses, we read that He will teach us. Not that we will figure them out ourselves, but that He will teach us. There is a considerable difference.

We noted in our introductory Bible passage that God, made His ways known to Moses but not to the people. The people that Moses led never did understand God's ways, and most of them perished in the wilderness due to their continual failings. So, what was it about Moses that qualified him to be taught by God? And when did he learn? Here are some characteristics of Moses:

- He became a prince in Egypt when one of Pharaoh's daughters took him out of the basket in the Nile and adopted him. This gave him the exceptional privileges of wealth and status.

- He was highly educated in the best system in the world of his day.

- He was a strong and good leader.

- He was courageous.

Naturally speaking, a man with these credentials would unquestionably qualify for higher office. However, there have been many people in history who met these qualifications and yet did not know the ways of God. Some of them were actually evil. This confirms the Bible statements that we cannot learn God's ways of our own accord, so we need to look further into the character of Moses, because God looks not at outward appearances but at our hearts (1 Samuel 16:7).

There is a remarkable statement regarding Moses in Numbers 12:3. It says, "Now Moses was very humble, more than all men who were on the face of the earth." The King

James version uses the word "meek" instead of "humble", and what is so astounding is that there is only one other reference to someone being considered meek in the Bible. That reference is to the Lord Jesus himself (Matthew 11:29). Moses was in outstanding company!

Humility and meekness are qualities that God values in us. Certainly, He Himself is very humble, and He dwells with those who are humble (Isaiah 57:15). This is true of such saints in the Bible as Elijah, Elisha, Samuel, Paul, and John. All of them had a close walk with God and were privileged to know His power and were given considerable revelation of God's ways. In my own experience, there is a man I knew who was given extraordinary experiences with God, including going to heaven, seeing visions of future world events, and being privileged to see the Lord several times. In spite of these wonderful experiences, one of the qualities that I observed in him was humility. His experiences surpassed anything that I have heard about in the lives of other people, but he was always so humble regarding them. Humility, then, is an essential quality if we are to learn the ways of God and perhaps more than anything else, this is what qualified Moses.

What other qualities do we see in Moses? For one, he was a faithful and reliable servant. For example, God told him to be sure to build the tabernacle exactly after the pattern that he had been shown. The tabernacle was not just a meeting house. It was the place where God dwelt among His people. Moreover, there is revelation regarding the nature of God in its measurements and its structure. God instructed Moses to construct the tabernacle after the pattern that he had been shown, and if Moses had not followed God's instruction precisely, the revelation would have been non-existent. Worse still, perhaps God would have deemed it inappropriate for His dwelling place.

Another example is Moses' diligence in following the Lord through the desert. When the people refused to enter the Promised Land, their journey was extended by thirty-eight years, and throughout that time, we see Moses faithfully leading them through the way that God directed. Lesser men would have taken short cuts or even given up. But Moses loved God, and obeying Him never seemed to be a hardship.

In Hebrews, we are provided with another important insight regarding Moses. He valued being identified with his own people, the children of Israel, above the position that he held as a prince in Egypt (Hebrews 11:26). This showed great character, as most people would have happily accepted the life of a prince with its wealth and privileges. Moses, however, was actually willing to suffer what the writer to Hebrews terms, "The reproaches of Christ." He was a man with high principles.

We see the same love for the people following the incident when they made a golden calf in the desert to worship instead of worshiping God. This was a terrible sin, and Moses was greatly concerned about how God would respond, so much so that he offered to have his own name removed from the Book of Life if God would forgive the people. In spite of all the complaints against him and the difficulties that these people caused him, Moses loved them.

I do believe that our character is so very important in our relationship with God, and when you think about it, what can we take with us when we pass on from this life? Obviously not our body. We take our character, the person we have become.

God will provide opportunities to test our character because it is so important. How will we respond in circumstances where doing the right thing costs us in some way? To illustrate, I know of a situation where a man received payments for some services that were of a nature that he had not previously performed, and he accidentally concealed the payments from the IRS. I say accidentally because he had researched the matter, reading several articles about the regulations, to see if these services were taxable but being unfamiliar with some of the terminology, he misinterpreted the articles. As a result, he believed the services were not taxable. This continued for a total of three years before he came to realize that he had made a mistake. The tax that should have been paid had now grown to become what was for him a fairly large sum.

It was an honest mistake with no intent to avoid the tax, and it happened that there was no documentation available to the IRS regarding the payments to him for these services. Therefore, if the man would be silent about the matter, he could keep the tax and no one would know. No one that is except God. The man believed that paying the tax was what he should do before God, and he regarded being in right standing with God as more important than the money. So, he voluntarily filed amended tax returns for the three years and paid the tax with interest. What would Moses have done had he been in that same situation? I'll let you think about it and decide.

The story had an interesting conclusion. The man paid the taxes for all three years but without his knowing, the IRS had previously reviewed one of the years and considered it closed. It happened that this was the year with the highest tax, almost half of the total, and because they had closed that year, the IRS refunded the money. God extended His kindness to the man.

We are considering Moses and how God taught him His ways. Moses was a truly remarkable man. He spoke with God face to face. He appeared on the Mount of Transfiguration, talking to Jesus and Elijah. The most astonishing of miracles were performed through him. However, these are the results of His relationship with God, not the basis.

So, what actually qualified Moses to be taught the ways of God?

As we have seen, he loved God deeply.

His attitude toward God was one of utter reverence.

He was obedient in all that God required of him, except for the instance when he struck the rock instead of speaking to it.

He loved God's people.

He exhibited exceptionally high character.

He was truly humble.

No doubt these were at least some of the reasons why God could teach Moses His ways. If we desire to be taught the ways of God, we can begin by emulating Moses.

When we boil it all down, Moses wanted the Lord to be honored, worshiped, and obeyed. That is how he was at the bottom of his heart.

What about us? We can ask ourselves, do we have the same qualities as Moses? If not, will we work on improving in them, with God's help? What is at the bottom of our hearts? How important is it to us to learn the ways of God?

Moses never deviated in his walk with God. When we compare this to the oscillating of the people, who were constantly influenced by their circumstances rather than God's promises and commands, we quickly realize the importance of knowing God's ways. This is not just something nice, some attribute that elevates us above most other people. No, it is a vital ingredient to becoming the man or woman that God intended us to become so that we fulfill His plan for our life. Hopefully, this book has encouraged you to diligently seek to understand the ways of God. As the writer to Hebrews noted, He is a rewarder of those who diligently seek Him.

www.ingramcontent.com/pod-product-compliance
Lightning Source LLC
Chambersburg PA
CBHW030456010526
44118CB00011B/971